To _____

From _____

Other books by Exley:
Daughters …
Missing You …
True Love …

Published simultaneously in 1995 by Exley Publications in Great Britain, and
Exley Giftbooks in the USA.
Copyright © Helen Exley 1995

12 11 10 9 8 7 6 5 4 3 2 1

Border illustrations by Juliette Clarke
Edited and pictures selected by Helen Exley

ISBN 1-85015-691-3

Designed by Pinpoint Design.
Picture research by P. A. Goldberg and J. M. Clift, Image Select, London.
Typeset by Delta, Watford.
Printed and bound by Tien Wah Ltd., Singapore

Exley Publications Ltd, 16 Chalk Hill, Watford, Herts. WD1 4BN.
Exley Giftbooks, 232 Madison Avenue, Suite 1206, NY 10016, USA.

SISTERS...

QUOTATIONS SELECTED BY
*H*ELEN EXLEY

EXLEY
NEW YORK · WATFORD UK

... if we believed the media we would think the only significant relationship in our lives is a romantic one. Yet sisterhood is probably the one that will last longer than any other.... A husband comes and goes, but a sister will always be around. She is someone to look up to, not for shallow reasons, like worldly success, but for their sensitivity and sensibility.

JANE DOWDESWELL,
FROM *"SISTERS ON SISTERS"*

What's a sister?
someone to confide in,
a girl that bosses you about,
a person that sides with you,
a friend for life,
a younger mother,
someone who hogs the shower,
smells like a chemist shop,
a person who's understanding,
That's a sister!!!

LOUISE DYE, AGE 11

Both within the family and without,
our sisters hold up our mirrors:
our images of who we are
and of who we can dare to become.

ELIZABETH FISHEL,
FROM "*SISTERS: LOVE AND RIVALRY*"

Sisters are connected throughout their lives by a
special bond – whether they try to ignore it or
not. For better or for worse, sisters remain sisters,
until death do them part.

BRIGID McCONVILLE, FROM "SISTERS: LOVE AND
CONFLICT WITHIN THE LIFELONG BOND"

Brothers and sisters are as close as
hands and feet.

VIETNAMESE PROVERB

Whatever you do they will love you; even if they
don't love you they are connected to you till you
die. You can be boring and tedious with sisters,
whereas you have to put on a good face with
friends.

DEBORAH MOGGACH, b.1948

The desire to be and have a sister is a primitive and profound one that may have everything or nothing to do with the family a woman is born to. It is a desire to know and be known by someone who shares blood and body, history and dreams, common ground and the unknown adventures of the future, darkest secrets and the glassiest beads of truth.

ELIZABETH FISHEL,
FROM *"SISTERS: LOVE AND RIVALRY"*

$\mathscr{D}$espite my underlying resentment, my sister's presence always mattered. How happy I was to see her waiting outside school for me the day I got my first report card. How crushed I was the night my friend Ellen and I put on "The Pajama Game" for our families and Susan was out with her friends....

NANCY KELTON

... my rock – I could never find a friend
who would give so much.

JESSICA MARTIN, 25

... the only person I'd give my last Rolo to.

HANNAH, 23

... dependent on me,
and I wouldn't want it any other way.

JAYNE IRVING, 31

... my confidante, my best friend, my ally.

JULIE, 32

... the one person who tolerated me,
defended me, played with me, *
whereas friends are often 'fair weather' friends.
She was always there.

SYLVIA, 63

... my memory – she brings back to life all our
happy childhood days, she makes me feel secure.

MARY, 76

collected by Jane Dowdeswell
from her book *"Sisters on Sisters"*

Often, in old age, they become each other's chosen and most happy companions. In addition to their shared memories of childhood and of their relationship to each other's children, they share memories of the same home, the same homemaking style, and the same small prejudices about housekeeping that carry the echoes of their mother's voice.

MARGARET MEAD (1901-1978).
FROM *"BLACKBERRY WINTER"*

… we never found again
That childish world where our
two spirits mingled
Like scents from varying roses
that remain
One sweetness, nor can evermore
be singled.

GEORGE ELIOT
[MARY ANN EVANS] (1819-1880),
FROM *"SCHOOL PARTED US"*

You can't think how I depend upon you, and when you're not there the colour goes out of my life, as water from a sponge; and I merely exist, dry and dusty. This is the exact truth: but not a very beautiful illustration of my complete adoration of you; and longing to sit, even saying nothing, and look at you.

VIRGINIA WOOLF (1882-1941),
TO VANESSA BELL

We shared. Parents. Home. Pets.
Celebrations. Catastrophes. Secrets.
And the threads of our experience
became so interwoven that we are
linked. I can never be utterly lonely,
knowing you share the planet. I need
news of you. I need to know you're
safe. I need you.

PAM BROWN, b.1928

For when three sisters love each other with such sincere affection, the one does not experience sorrow, pain, or affliction of any kind, but the others' heart wishes to relieve, and vibrates in tenderness. Like a well-organized musical instrument.

ELIZABETH SHAW, *SISTER OF ABIGAIL ADAMS AND MARY CRANCH*

*Children
of the same
mother*

*do not always
agree.*

NIGERIAN PROVERB

He hit me on the face, Mummy
so I hit him back

He hit me on the leg, Mummy
so I hit him back

He hit me on the back, Mummy
so I hit him back on the back

He hurlded me, Mummy
so I hurlded him back

He was the one who started it, Mummy
so I started it back.

LESLEY MIRANDA

We may be stars to the world, but we are not stars to one another. We are just sisters. One will make quite clear to the other two that they cannot be stars on their own. One Beverley Sister is useless. Two Beverley Sisters are useless. Only three Beverley Sisters are stars.
Divided – we fall.

THE BEVERLEY SISTERS

Sugar and spice and all things nice.
Perhaps. To an outsider.
… Siblings are more realistic. To them a
sister is naggings and needlings, whispers
and whisperings. Bribery Thumpings.
Borrowings. Breakings.
Kisses and cuddlings. Lendings. Surprises.
Defendings and comfortings.
Welcomings home.

PAM BROWN, b. 1928

But however you might rebel, there was no shedding them. They were your responsibility and there was no one to relieve you of them. They called you Sis. All your life people called you Sis, because that was what you were, or what you became — big sister, helpful sister, the one upon whom everyone depended, the one they all came to for everything from help with homework to a sliver under the fingernail.

WALLACE STEGNER

OLDER SISTERS ... are liable to nag. To refuse to lend you things. To scold. To make you walk too fast.

But, on the other hand, they take on bully boys at school and send them running for their lives.

They disentangle problems in arithmetic and knitting.

And when they're grown they listen to your secrets and anxieties. And never tell – without your say-so.

An older sister is a friend and a defender – a listener, conspirator, a counsellor and a sharer of delights.

And sorrows too.

A YOUNGER SISTER ... is a valuable addition to a boy's life.

Someone to send ahead to test the tussocks in the marsh. Someone to use as guinea pig in trying sledges and experimental go-carts.

But someone who needs you – who comes to you with bumped heads, grazed knees, tales of persecution.

Someone who trusts you to defend her.

Someone who thinks you know the answers to almost everything.

PAM BROWN, b.1928

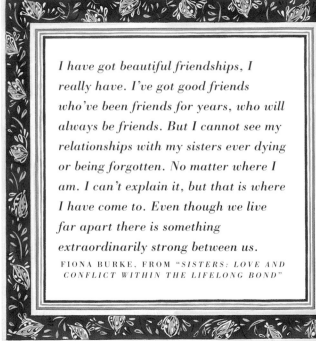

I have got beautiful friendships, I really have. I've got good friends who've been friends for years, who will always be friends. But I cannot see my relationships with my sisters ever dying or being forgotten. No matter where I am. I can't explain it, but that is where I have come to. Even though we live far apart there is something extraordinarily strong between us.

FIONA BURKE, FROM "*SISTERS: LOVE AND CONFLICT WITHIN THE LIFELONG BOND*"

*M*ost relationships – friendships, love affairs, marriages – require a certain amount of servicing to keep them ticking over. When a year or so passes without having heard from friends, people tend to say they have "lost touch". If couples so much as part to take a holiday, eyebrows tend to be raised, while most relatives expect the occasional phone call or Christmas card at least.

Yet the sisters' relationship seems to be a dramatic exception. For many sisters, the bond which is forged in childhood is not only durable, but it hardly requires any formal attention in the great gaps of time and space that often separate them in adult life. "Losing touch" generally isn't an issue.

BRIGID McCONVILLE, FROM *"SISTERS: LOVE AND CONFLICT WITHIN THE LIFELONG BOND"*

A sibling is any other kid your mother and father have around the house. You will not like him (her). He (she) will not like you. Make friends with him (her) anyhow. It evens up the odds with your parents.

ROBERT PAUL SMITH

I might have seen more of America when I was a child if I hadn't had to spend so much of my time protecting my half of the back seat from incursions by sister, Sukey.

CALVIN TRILLIN

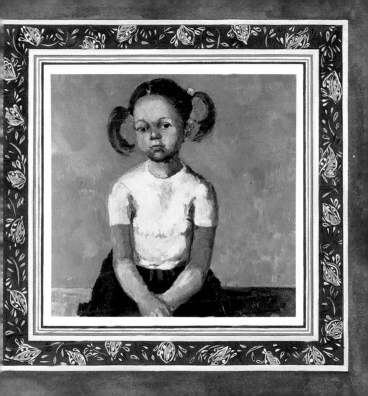

Ties

Father, mother,
Sister, brother,
Tied one to all,
Each to each other.

Ties that bind
Like solid steel,
Ties you can't see,
Only feel.

Travel far
And then you'll know
Ties that bind
And won't let go.

Father, mother,
Sister, brother,
Tied one to all,
Each to each other.

TONY
BRADMAN

*Y*our sister is … the one person you will probably know for longer than any other. Whether that is as your strength, a lifeline, a best friend, or as your biggest enemy depends on the sister! When you're growing up, a sister can be a readymade playmate; as a teenager,

you've got a live-in counsellor, as a
mother, you've got an automatic
auntie and willing babysitter, in
old age, you've got someone who
doesn't get bored by all your
stories of the "good old days".

JANE DOWDESWELL
FROM "SISTERS ON SISTERS"

Thank you for trying to keep me out of trouble — for cleaning me up when I fell in the cowpat, for drying me out when I followed the ducks into the pond, for wheedling me down when I was stuck in the oak tree, for stitching the jacket I ripped scrambling through barbed wire, for drying out the book Mum said I wasn't to read in the bath.

She always found out of course.

But thanks for trying.

PAM BROWN, b. 1928

Jealousy and love are sisters.

RUSSIAN PROVERB

*Big sisters are the crab grass
in the lawn of life.*

CHARLES M. SCHULZ, b.1922

*The young ladies
entered the drawing room
in the full fervour
of sisterly animosity.*

ROBERT SMITH SURTEES (1803-1864),
FROM "MR. SPONGE'S SPORTING TOUR"

You can kid the world.
But not your sister.

CHARLOTTE GRAY, b.1937

If your sister
is in a tearing hurry to go out
and cannot catch your eye,
she's wearing your
best sweater.

PAM BROWN, b.1928

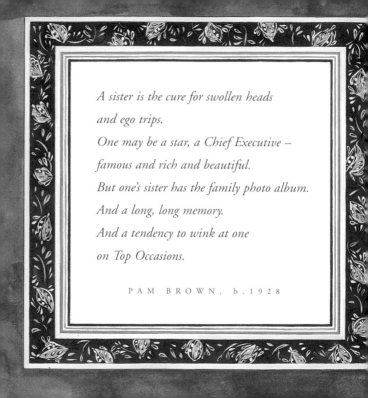

A sister is the cure for swollen heads
and ego trips.
One may be a star, a Chief Executive –
famous and rich and beautiful.
But one's sister has the family photo album.
And a long, long memory.
And a tendency to wink at one
on Top Occasions.

PAM BROWN, b.1928

$\mathcal{W}$e share a mutual knowledge of the intuitive, unspoken kind. So that when I think of each sister, there is something essential which I know about her in a way I could never describe to an outsider. It is like having a sixth sense, or a perception of someone's aura.

BRIGID McCONVILLE,
FROM "SISTERS. LOVE AND CONFLICT WITHIN THE LIFELONG BOND"

How could I be jealous of her? Everything she has she shares with me. I had a life-threatening illness just about the time she started to make it in TV. I had just come out of a coma when she came to the hospital and leaned over my bed and whispered, "Little Mich, little Mich, don't you worry about anything. Wherever I go, I'll take care of you." And she has.

MICHIE NADER

For there is no friend like a sister,

In calm or stormy weather;

To cheer one on the tedious way,

To fetch one if one goes astray,

To lift one if one totters down,

To strengthen whilst one stands.

CHRISTINA ROSSETTI (1830-1894),
FROM "GOBLIN MARKET"

I played with you 'mid cowslips
   blowing,
When I was six and you were four;
When garlands weaving,
   flower-balls throwing,
Were pleasures soon to please no
   more.
Through groves and meads, o'er
   grass and heather,
With little playmates, to and fro,
We wandered hand in hand
   together;
But that was sixty years ago.

T . L . P E A C O C K

I cannot deny that, now I am without your company I feel not only that I am deprived of a very dear sister, but that I have lost half of myself.

BEATRICE D'ESTE,
IN A LETTER TO HER SISTER ISABELLA

Sisters are our peers,
the voice of our times.

ELIZABETH FISHEL

I *have* lost a treasure, such a Sister, such a friend, as never can have been surpassed, – she was the sun of my life, the gilder of every pleasure, the soother of every sorrow, I had not a thought conccaled from her, & it is as if I had lost a part of myself. I loved her only too well, not better than she deserved, but I am conscious that my affection for her made me sometimes unjust to and negligent of others.

CASSANDRA AUSTEN TO FANNY KNIGHT,
FROM *"LETTERS"*

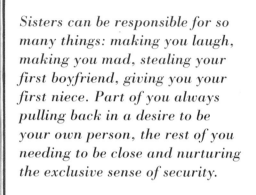

Sisters can be responsible for so many things: making you laugh, making you mad, stealing your first boyfriend, giving you your first niece. Part of you always pulling back in a desire to be your own person, the rest of you needing to be close and nurturing the exclusive sense of security.

JANE DOWDESWELL,
FROM "SISTERS ON SISTERS"

You keep your past by having sisters. As you get older they're the only ones who don't get bored if you talk about your memories. It's like when you meet someone who's been to India, and you have too; you can talk for hours. Everyone else around you is bored but you're totally enthralled by each other's words. It's like that with sisters.

DEBORAH MOGGACH, b.1948

Acknowledgements: The publishers are grateful for permission to reproduce copyright material. While every effort has been made to trace copyright holders, the publishers would be pleased to hear from any not here acknowledged. TONY BRADMAN: "Ties" from "You Just Can't Win", published by Blackie, 1991, © Tony Bradman, reprinted by permission of Rogers, Coleridge and White. FIONA BURKE: extract from "Sisters: Love and Conflict Within the Lifelong Bond" published by Pan Books, a division of Pan Macmillan Ltd., © 1985 Brigid McConville; JANE DOWDESWELL: extracts from "Sister on Sisters" published by Grapevine/Thorsons, a division of HarperCollins Publishers Ltd., 1988; ELIZABETH FISHEL: extracts from "Sisters: Love and Rivalry Inside the Family and Beyond", 1979; BRIGID McCONVILLE: extracts from "Sisters: Love and Conflict Within the Lifelong Bond", published by Pan Books, a division of Pan Macmillan Ltd., © 1985 Brigid McConville, reprinted by permission of Sheil Land Associates. MARGARET MEAD: extract from "Blackberry Winter: My Earlier Years". Reprinted by permission of Angus and Robertson, an imprint of HarperCollins Publishers Ltd. and William Morrow and Co. Inc.; LESLEY MIRANDA: "Don't Hit Your Sister" taken from "Black Poetry", compiled by Grace Nichols, published by Blackie, 1988; VIRGINIA WOOLF: extract from "The Letters of Virginia Woolf", published by Harcourt Brace, © 1976 Quentin Bell and Angelica Garnett.

Picture Credits: Exley Publications is very grateful to the following individuals and organizations for permission to reproduce their pictures: